The Life Cycle of a
Salmon
by Lisa Trumbauer

Consulting Editor: Gail Saunders-Smith, Ph.D.

Consultant: Thomas P. Quinn, Professor,
School of Aquatic and Fish Sciences,
University of Washington

Pebble Books

an imprint of Capstone Press
Mankato, Minnesota

Pebble Books are published by Capstone Press
151 Good Counsel Drive, P.O. Box 669, Mankato, Minnesota 56002
http://www.capstone-press.com

1 2 3 4 5 6 07 06 05 04 03 02

Library of Congress Cataloging-in-Publication Data
Trumbauer, Lisa, 1963–
   The life cycle of a salmon / by Lisa Trumbauer.
   p. cm.—(Life cycles)
   Includes bibliographical references (p. 23) and index.
   Summary: Simple text and photographs present the life cycle of the salmon.
   ISBN 0-7368-1453-1 (hardcover)
   1. Salmon—Life cycles—Juvenile literature. [1. Salmon.] I. Title. II. Life cycles
(Mankato, Minn.)
QL638.S2 T825 2003
597.5′6—dc21   2002001227

Note to Parents and Teachers

The Life Cycles series supports national science standards related
to life science. This book describes and illustrates the life cycle
of a sockeye salmon. The photographs support early readers in
understanding the text. The repetition of words and phrases helps
early readers learn new words. This book also introduces early
readers to subject-specific vocabulary words, which are defined
in the Words to Know section. Early readers may need assistance
to read some words and to use the Table of Contents, Words to
Know, Read More, Internet Sites, and Index/Word List sections
of the book.

Table of Contents

Photographs in this book show the life cycle
of a sockeye salmon.

1 day

A salmon begins life
as an egg in a river.

6 months

An alevin hatches from the egg. The alevin gets its food from the yolk.

1 year

The alevin becomes a fry.
It lives with other fry
in large schools.

2 years

The fry becomes a smolt.
The smolt migrates
downriver to the ocean.

4 years

The smolt becomes
an adult. Salmon live in
the ocean for two to
three years.

14

Then the salmon migrates again. It returns to the river where it hatched.

The female salmon gets ready to spawn. She digs a hole with her tail. She lays eggs in the hole.

The male salmon fertilizes the eggs. The male and female salmon die after spawning.

alevin

fry

eggs

smolt

adult

20

The eggs are the start of a new life cycle.

(Words to Know

alevin—the second stage of a salmon's life; an alevin looks like a small fish with a food pouch.

egg—the first stage of a salmon's life; an egg is small and round.

fertilize—to join an egg of a female with a sperm of a male to produce young

fry—the third stage of a salmon's life; a fry looks like a small, silver fish.

life cycle—the stages of life of an animal; the life cycle includes being born, growing up, having young, and dying.

migrate—to travel from one area to another

school—a large group of fish; schools of fry often live in lakes.

smolt—the fourth stage of a salmon's life; a smolt looks similar to an adult.

spawn—to produce many young; a female salmon can spawn up to 4,000 eggs at once.

Read More

Crewe, Sabrina. *The Salmon*. Life Cycles. Austin, Texas: Raintree Steck-Vaughn, 1997.

Hirschi, Ron. *Salmon*. Minneapolis: Carolrhoda Books, 2001.

Martin-James, Kathleen. *Swimming Salmon*. Pull Ahead Books. Minneapolis: Lerner Publishing, 2003.

Internet Sites

Salmon Life Cycle
http://www.ecy.wa.gov/programs/sea/
pugetsound/species/salmon_cyc.html

Salmon Life Cycle Printout/Quiz
http://www.enchantedlearning.com/subjects/
fish/printouts/salmon.shtml

The Salmon Story
http://www.cf.adfg.state.ak.us/geninfo/
research/genetics/kids/salstory.htm

Index/Word List

Word Count: 121
Early-Intervention Level: 15

Editorial Credits
Martha E. H. Rustad, editor; Kia Adams, cover designer; Jennifer Schonborn, interior
  designer; Wanda Winch, photo researcher; Karen Risch, product planning editor

Photo Credits
AP Photo/Barry Sweet, 12
Bruce Coleman Inc./Jeff Foott, cover (right), 6, 16, 20 (alevin)
Gregory Ruggerone, 8, 14, 20 (fry)
Minden Pictures/Matthias Breiter, 1
Thomas P. Quinn, 4, 18, 20 (eggs and adult)
Wet Waders, Inc./Mark Emery, cover (left), 10, 20 (smolt)